Simple Flower Style

Simple Flower Style

Fresh Arrangements for Today's Home

Paige Gilchrist

LARK BOOKS

A Division of Sterling Publishing Co., Inc.
New York

Editor: PAIGE GILCHRIST

Art Director: DANA IRWIN

Cover Designer: BARBARA ZARETSKY

Photographers: SANDRA STAMBAUGH,
RICHARD HASSELBERG

Assistant Editors: VERONIKA ALICE GUNTER
AND HEATHER SMITH

Editorial Assistant: RAIN NEWCOMB

Editorial Intern: ANNE WOLFF HOLLYFIELD

Assistant Art Director: HANNES CHAREN

SPECIAL PHOTOGRAPHY

Sanoma Syndication

Jack Aarts

Robbert Hans Beck

Mirjam Bleeker

Dennis Brandsma

Studio Cameron

John Dummer

Hotze Eisma

Renee Frinking

Luuk Geertsen

Rene Gonkel

John van Groenedaal

Paul Grootes

Peter Kooijman

Lois Lemaire

Eric van Lokven

Robert Mulder

Otto Polman

Pia van Spaendonck

Jeroen van der Spek

Dolf Straatemeier

Rob van Uchelen

Carel Verduin

George v.d. Wijngaard

Hans Zeegers

Library of Congress Cataloging-in-Publication Data

Gilchrist, Paige.
    Simple flower style : fresh arrangements for today's
home / by Paige Gilchrist.
       p. cm.
    ISBN 1-57990-295-2 (hard)
    1. Flower arrangement. I. Title.

SB449 .G53 2002
745.92—dc21

                                        2001050325

10 9 8 7 6 5 4 3 2 1

First Edition

Published by Lark Books, a division of
Sterling Publishing Co., Inc.
387 Park Avenue South, New York, N.Y. 10016

© 2002, Lark Books

Distributed in Canada by Sterling Publishing,
c/o Canadian Manda Group, One Atlantic Ave., Suite
105, Toronto, Ontario, Canada M6K 3E7

Distributed in the U.K. by Guild of Master Craftsman
Publications Ltd., Castle Place, 166 High Street, Lewes,
East Sussex, England BN7 1XU
Tel: (+ 44) 1273 477374, Fax: (+ 44) 1273 478606,
Email: pubs@thegmcgroup.com, Web: www.gmcpublica-
tions.com

Distributed in Australia by Capricorn Link (Australia) Pty
Ltd., P.O. Box 704, Windsor, NSW 2756 Australia

The written instructions, photographs, designs, patterns,
and projects in this volume are intended for the person-
al use of the reader and may be reproduced for that
purpose only. Any other use, especially commercial use,
is forbidden under law without written permission of the
copyright holder.

Every effort has been made to ensure that all the information in this book is accurate. However, due to differ-
ing conditions, tools, and individual skills, the publisher
cannot be responsible for any injuries, losses, and other
damages that may result from the use of the information
in this book.

If you have questions or comments about this book,
please contact:
Lark Books
67 Broadway
Asheville, NC 28801
(828) 236-9730

Printed in Hong Kong

ISBN 1-57990-295-2

CONTENTS

Introduction   6

SIMPLE FLOWER STYLE BASICS
Tools, materials, care, maintenance   9

SINGLE BLOOMS
Displaying just one or one type   20

COMBINATIONS
Easy ways to start mixing it up   33

SHAPE & SCALE
Playing with the form and size of flowers and displays   43

COLOR
Hot, pale, contrasting, harmonious—showing off flower shades   63

SETTINGS
Displays that have to do with where you put them   76

CONTAINERS
How the container you choose helps make the look   90

HOLDING IT ALL TOGETHER
Frogs, rocks, wraps, ties—decorative ways to hold flowers in place   116

Contributors   128
Acknowledgments   128
Index   128

INTRODUCTION

TRY TO CAPTURE IN WORDS WHAT IT IS ABOUT FLOWERS

that captivates human beings so, and the poets among us say they're everything from the darlings of the gods

and the hieroglyphics of angels to the earth's laughter and the tools of nature's courtship. We've been putting flowers on exhibit since ancient times, using them to adorn the heads of heroes and the statues of gods and goddesses, decorate the waters of baths, and dress the centers of banquet tables. Today, we count on flowers to perform all sorts of duties: perk up drab spaces, give parties life, set the mood

for meals, and act as conversation pieces. How nice to know, in the midst of increasingly busy lives, that they can do all of that with very little effort on our part.

WHEN WE SAY SIMPLE FLOWER STYLE, WE MEAN IT

People who publish books often feel obliged to turn some of life's most basic pleasures into elaborate undertakings that closely resemble work. An afternoon walk in the woods becomes a hiking expedition (chapters on maps, compasses, outdoor gear). Dinner for friends, a multicourse production (sections on place cards, linens, and the wonders of which fork goes where).

We hope you won't feel cheated, but we think there are certain subjects that simply shouldn't be that difficult. The impulse to pluck or purchase

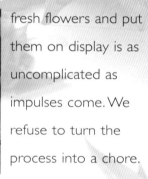

fresh flowers and put them on display is as uncomplicated as impulses come. We refuse to turn the process into a chore.

THE BEST OF BOTH WORLDS

Ask today's hottest floral designers about new trends in flower fashion, and they'll gush about how East has met West. They'll say they see a fusion of the world's two great floral traditions—the extravagant abundance of Western style and the restrained formality of Eastern arrangements—resulting in a new, relaxed blend. What all this excitement means for the average person who wants to put a few flowers in a vase is that simple, casual styles are now not only easier and more suited to your setting, they're in.

Rather than depending on elaborate techniques, these modern looks celebrate the distinctive characteristics of flowers themselves—maybe the lush shape of a lily or the blazing tangerine of a parrot tulip—and the creative ways those flowers can interact with each other, their containers, and the places you put them.

Examples, Examples, Examples

We give you 80 gorgeous ones, ranging from sweet to graphic to brilliantly energetic: daisies peeking out of vintage soda bottles, single white roses wired to river stones, a

spray of purple rhododendron bursting out of an electric-green martini pitcher. Though the displays are easy to duplicate, if you like (simple instructions accompany each), not a single one requires that you use exactly the flower or container we do. Frankly, they don't even require that you know the difference between a peony and a petunia—only that you know what you like. You get to improvise your own rules in this new floral global village.

Anything Goes, but a Few Basics Still Apply

The Zen minimalism of a single sprig in a small black vase is fine. So is a flashy bunch of tropical blooms—and most everything in-between. What gives all these displays  their contemporary flair is that they look as if they were casually tossed together rather than formally arranged. The truth, however, is that even the

simplest creations benefit from some basic principles of flower arranging and care, so we give you a handy overview of those, too—everything from how to choose the right vase shape to ways to revive sagging stems.

Use this book as a guide to today's new flower styles. Use it for inspiration. Most of all, use it as a  reminder that placing a flower in a vase was never meant to be a complicated undertaking, but merely a happy bit of play with the darlings of the gods.

SIMPLE
FLOWER
STYLE BASICS

THE CHARM OF TODAY'S SIMPLE FLOWER

STYLES IS THAT THEY LOOK SO EFFORT-

LESS. THE JOY OF THEM IS THAT THEY ARE.

A HANDFUL OF STANDARD SUPPLIES AND

A FEW EASY TECHNIQUES ARE ALL YOU

NEED TO CREATE THESE CASUAL DISPLAYS.

MATERIALS & TOOLS

Knife. A sharp, clean, all-purpose knife will come in handy for cutting, slicing, and scraping flower stems.

Clippers. For cutting through tough stems and twigs, you need a pair of heavy-duty clippers. Lighter clippers are good for detail work, such as nipping dead blooms.

Scissors. Household scissors can handle some of the same jobs light clippers are made for. They're also what you need for cutting ribbon, raffia, string, and other items you might use in your arrangements.

Loppers. If you like to include flowering branches in your displays, you'll use loppers to prune them.

Chicken wire and flower frogs. These holding devices help keep your flowers upright and in place. Crumpled chicken wire pushed down into the bottom of a vase provides an excellent support for stems. Frogs, which you can choose to make a visible part of your arrangement, come in a wide range of sizes, shapes, and styles, including those with spikes, deep wells, and thick metal mesh.

Floral foam. It's not best for heavy stems, but floral foam, which is typically green and comes in a variety of shapes, will help hold lighter blooms in place, especially in shallow arrangements. Do note, though, that it tends to clog stems. Flowers arranged in floral foam won't last as long as those that have direct access to water, so use it only when it's necessary. Saturate the foam before using

it by floating it in a container of water, letting it absorb the moisture naturally. It's fully saturated when it sinks and air bubbles stop rising to the surface. This usually takes about 30 minutes. Don't over soak your foam, or it may disintegrate.

Florist's tape. Use this waterproof tape, available in both green and clear, to secure floral foam to the vase of a container, to create a stem-holding grid across the mouth of a vase, or for any other simple adhering of one part of an arrangement to another.

Florist's wire. You can straighten stems or bind one flower to another almost imperceptibly with thin florist's wire.

Water mister. Like any living being, flowers benefit from regular hydration, and all parts of a flower take in water. A mister is good for lightly spritzing flower heads.

BUYING FLOWERS

One of the most important things to look for if you're buying your flowers is a busy flower shop. Not only is the steady stream of customers a good sign that others have been happy with the flowers they've purchased there in the past, but it also means inventory tends to go out the door quickly, so the flowers the shop has in stock are likely quite fresh. Beyond that, take a good look at the shop's flowers themselves. The petals shouldn't have bruises and should feel crisp, not limp, between your fingers. Stems should be firm and green rather than dark and slimy. In general, the flowers shouldn't look faded or wilted. Once you're satisfied with the overall quality, choose flowers that are neither too tightly closed (tight, green buds will probably never open) nor too fully open (they've already hit their peak). If you're buying flowers for a specific event, try to do so a day or two in advance, picking loosely closed flowers. They should open to full bloom just in time. If you're picking up foliage, too, choose stalks that aren't wilting or turning yellow or brown. Most commercially grown flowers should last for about five days, though especially fragile and delicate varieties may have a shorter life span.

HARVESTING FLOWERS

Whether you have a well-planned cutting garden or just a happy patch of flowering shrubs that came with your yard, during the growing season you may be able to cut much of what you need for flower arrangements yourself. Try to harvest your flowers in the early part of the day, before the sun zaps their internal water supply. Whatever the time, take a bucket of water with you, and plunge the stems in it immediately after cutting them. Choose flowers that aren't quite in full bloom; they'll last longer once they're cut. And leave new buds alone. They'll quickly become limp in a display, but left in place they'll produce blooms for your next arrangement.

CONDITIONING

We ask a lot of cut flowers, expecting them to look perky and bright long after we've deprived them of their natural source of nutrients and

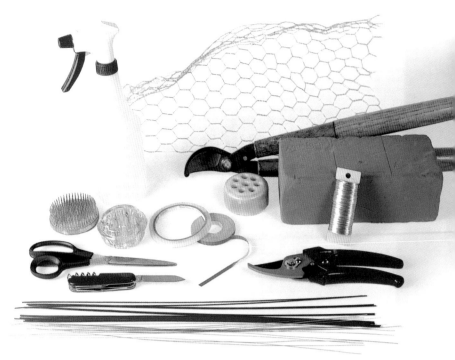

water. The least we can do is help them adjust. That's what basic conditioning techniques do.

CUTTING

As soon as you get your flowers home or inside, give all the stems a fresh cut on a diagonal. When they're placed in their container, the flowers will rest on the point of the cut rather than flat, leaving room for water to flow up the stem. Also, strip off any leaves that will be below the waterline in the arrangement; leaves submerged in water will rot quickly, and most flowers do better if they're not competing with their own foliage for water. At the same time, remove any damaged petals and snip off any thorns on the stems.

If you have time, let your recut flowers sit in a temporary container in a cool, dark place overnight, so they can take a good, long drink. This process, called hardening, ensures that the flowers absorb as much water as possible before they begin sealing off their pores.

Clockwise from top left: water mister, chicken wire, loppers, floral foam, spooled florist's wire, clippers, straight florist's wire, knife, scissors, frogs, and florist's tape

FEEDING & WATERING

When you submerge your flower stems, whether to harden them overnight or for the final arrangement, use tepid water. It's easier for oxygen to travel through on its way up the stems. Adding floral food will nourish your flowers, encourage buds to develop, and help prevent bacteria from growing. You can mix your own by dissolving a capful of bleach and a couple of small spoonfuls of sugar in a gallon (3.8 L) of water. Most critical, however, is that you change the water regularly, keeping it clean and sparkling.

TREATING STEMS

Different types of stems benefit from specific conditioning.

Hollow-stemmed flowers, such as amaryllis and delphinium, need to stay full of water. Use a watering can to fill the stems, then plug them with cotton.

Woody-stemmed flowers, such as the branches of lilacs and forsythia, are better able to draw water if you split the stem vertically with clippers or a sharp knife from the base to about an inch or two (2 to 5 cm) up.

Milky-stemmed flowers, such as poppies and hollyhocks, exude a milky substance from their cut stems that taints water, and losing the milk deprives the flowers of nutrients. Sear the ends of milky stems briefly to seal the nutrients in.

Stems with nodes, such as carnations, need to be cut between the nodes of the stalks, so they can more easily draw water.

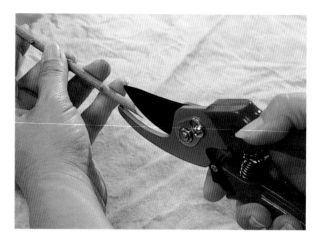

Splitting a woody stem

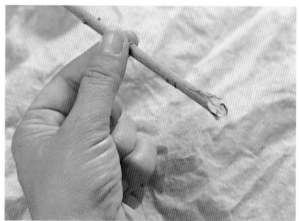

Searing a milky stem

REMOVING STAMENS

The prominent, pollen-coated stamens of flowers such as lilies can stain clothing, and, some say, deprive the flowers of water, causing them to wilt sooner. If you like, snip the stamens out with small scissors before you start arranging your flowers.

REVIVING WILTED FLOWERS

If the trip from flower shop to home—or even from garden to inside—occurs on an especially hot day, your flower heads and stems may be drooping by the time you're ready to arrange them. Standing them in water in a cool, dark place overnight, as described on page 9, will give most flowers a lift. But if yours are in more serious need of resuscitation, submerge them completely, heads, stems, and all, in a tub of tepid water for an hour or so. Weight them down just below the heads. This technique also helps revive color in some flowers.

STRAIGHTENING STEMS

Some flowers, including tulips, anemones, and gerberas, naturally have bent or crooked stems. In some arrangements, you may find this charming. In others, frustrating. You can encourage them to stiffen and straighten by wrapping a bundle of stems tightly together in a few sheets of newspaper, then placing them in a straight-sided container for an hour or two.

If you want even more control, wire each stem. Insert the end of a piece of florist's wire at the base of the flower head, then gently twist the wire around the stem. When you finish, trim off any extra wire at the end.

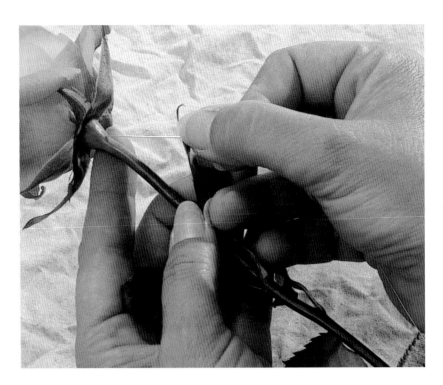

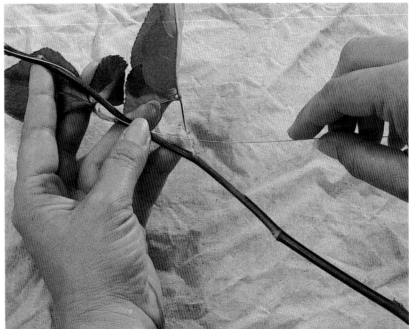

Wiring a stem to keep it straight

TAPING A STEM GRID

As you'll see in the Holding it All Together chapter, beginning on page 116, there are plenty of ways to incorporate the props that hold your flowers in place into your arrangement. If you prefer a holding mechanism that remains invisible, tape a stem grid over the mouth of your container. Run florist's tape across the mouth in a crisscross grid, basing the size of the grid's holes on the size of your flower stems, then stick your stems in the openings.

Using florist's tape to tape a stem grid

FORMING ARRANGEMENTS

If you're working with more than just a few flowers, you'll have more control if you form your arrangement in your hand or on a flat surface before transferring it to a container. Once you transfer it, fill in with additional flowers, if necessary. Following are three basic approaches you can apply to nearly any style of arrangement.

FORMING AN ARRANGEMENT IN YOUR HAND

Form the core of the arrangement with several stems in the crook of your hand.

Continue adding flowers in graduated heights around the core.

You end up with a full display surrounding a central peak.

Hold the arrangement up to your container to determine where to clip the ends of the stems.

FORMING AN ARRANGEMENT ON A FLAT SURFACE

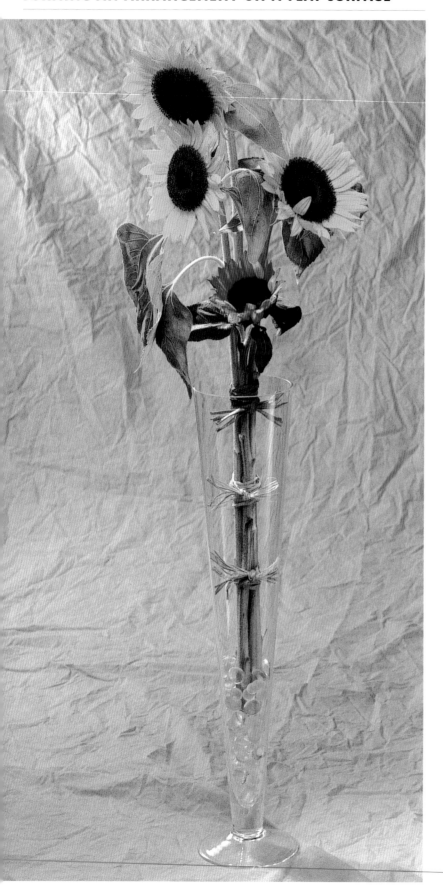

If you're working with large, heavy flowers, and/or if you're tying the stems as part of the display, start by laying the core of your arrangement on a flat surface, with the heads hanging over an edge, so they won't be crushed.

Fill in with additional flowers in graduated heights around the core.

Hold the arrangement up to your container to determine where to clip the ends of the stems before placing it in the container.

Tie the stems together, if you like.

WRAPPING AN ARRANGEMENT

Form the arrangement in your hand, then hold the stems in place with a rubber band.

Position the arrangement in the center of your wrap, whether it's a leaf, as shown here, decorative paper, or some other material. Add some foliage behind the flowers, if you like.

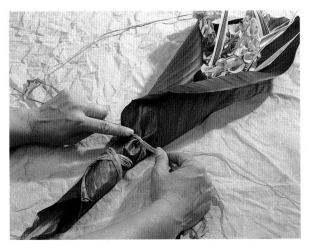

Fold in the wrap's edges, and secure them with twine, ribbon, raffia, even wire.

Hold the arrangement up to your container to determine where to clip the ends of the stems. You want them to stick out past the base of the wrap, so they can easily reach the water once you set the flowers in their container.

CARE

Start with good-quality flowers and prepare them well, and they should look lively for five days or so. In addition, there are a few simple ways you can help prolong the life of your arrangement.

❖ Position the arrangement away from hot sun, direct light, or cold drafts.

❖ Refill the container with fresh water daily. This doesn't mean you have to take the arrangement apart and reassemble it each time you change the water. Just stand the container in the sink under a running tap, and let the water flush out the old and refill the container. If your arrangement is simply too large to refill with clean water daily, at the very least top it off with a fresh splash each day.

❖ Pick off dead leaves and petals, and snip off faded or dead blossoms entirely.

❖ Remove wilted flowers and replace them with fresh ones, if possible.

❖ For a drastic overhaul, pick out the few flowers that still look cheerful, compost or discard the rest, and make a new, smaller arrangement.

FORCING INTO FLOWER

To force blooming sprays into early flower, submerge them in warm water to swell the buds, slit the stem ends, as described on page 12, and place them in warm water in a warm room. You can also persuade some flowers to open more fully. Gently coax the petals outward with your finger and thumb, and they'll hold the position.

CONTAINER CARE

The surest way to cause your flowers to decay prematurely is to arrange them in a dirty vase. Vases that aren't cleaned well can pass bacteria from one bouquet to another. Wash your vases and other containers with a mild bleach solution, using a bottle brush on narrow-necked vases. Rinse them thoroughly and dry them completely before storing them.

SINGLE BLOOMS

A SOLITARY BLOOM POSING ARTFULLY IN A VASE, OR A NO-FRILLS GROUPING OF A SINGLE FLOWER TYPE—NOTHING CAPTURES THE SPIRIT OF SIMPLE FLOWER STYLE BETTER. THESE UNCOMPLICATED PRESENTATIONS, WHICH CAN RANGE FROM DAINTY TO DARING, ARE QUICK, INEXPENSIVE, AND DELIGHTFULLY EASY. THEIR PURPOSE, AFTER ALL, IS TO SHOWCASE THE BEAUTY OF THE BLOSSOM, RATHER THAN THE VIRTUOSITY OF THE ARRANGER. YOUR MAIN JOB WITH SINGLE-BLOOM DISPLAYS IS TO MAKE SURE YOUR FLOWER IS WELL CONDITIONED BEFORE IT'S PLACED IN ITS CONTAINER (SEE PAGE 11) AND REGULARLY SUPPLIED WITH FRESH WATER AFTERWARD. THE REAL FUN, THOUGH, IS IN PLAYING ARCHITECT, SCULPTOR, AND COLOR THEORIST, MATCHING YOUR FLOWER WITH JUST THE RIGHT VASE, THEN PUTTING THE TWO TOGETHER IN THE PERFECT PLACE.

EVEN IF YOU DON'T REGULARLY RECEIVE A DOZEN ROSES, you've no doubt seen the classic tribute to true love on display— all the blooms clustered together in one big, predictable bunch. What a striking switch to unbundle them and stand the stems side by side in a precise row. Here, we keep our roses in line by placing them in test tubes snugged down in drilled holes in a long piece of lumber. They'd behave just as well, though, in shot glasses queued up on a windowsill or in old medicine bottles running down the center of the dining room table.

JAZZ MUSICIANS SAY IT'S THE EMPTY SPACES BETWEEN THE NOTES that add interest to a piece of music. Artful voids can also be just what you need to make a group of flowers sing. With top-heavy blooms such as the amaryllis here, you want a big, stable vase. But that doesn't mean you're obligated to fill it full. Loosely weave together the stems of just a few flowers as you position them in the water. The delicate balance of stem against stem holds everything in place, while leaving plenty of open patches for light to stream through.

YOU'VE GOT TO HAND IT TO THE VICTORIANS. Those inventors of everything from aspic knives to finger bowls knew how to assemble the right specialized accessories to make a pretty table. One of the best pieces of tableware they popularized was a cinch-waisted glass container called a forcing jar. Reproductions are available at florists, nurseries, and through mail-order catalogues today, making it easy—and dirt free—to create a simple tabletop garden out of flowering bulbs.

Fill the lower section of the jar with water to just below the cinch. Place your bulb (hyacinths, amaryllis, and paper whites all work well) on the upper section of the jar. You don't want the water touching the bulb, but it needs to be close enough for the bulb to "smell it," as veteran bulb forcers say. Settle the jar in a cool, dark place, such as an unheated garage, and keep the water level constant until the root system is well developed and the bulb has begun to sprout (typically 13 to 15 weeks). When the shoots are several inches tall, move everything to a location with low light and slightly warmer temperatures for a few days, then out to a sunny location where the bulb can bloom.

SOMETIMES, YOU WANT TO TAKE THE PRESSURE OFF COMPLETELY— for guests and

host alike. One of the best ways to eliminate flower-display pretension is to give yourself over

wholeheartedly to charm. Choose an unassuming work-horse flower like the sunny marigolds

we've used here. (*We've got a real job to do keeping pests out of the garden,* they seem to say.

Sitting pretty on a table is something we do only in our off hours.) Offset a couple of stems in a

bunch of small vases, and place one at each place setting. It's not at all necessary that your con-

tainers match. For a clean, coordinated look, simply make sure they're all the same color or clear.

HERE'S A HANDSOME LESSON IN SPATIAL RELATIONS. The more closely you match the size of the opening of your container to the diameter of your flower's stem, the better able you'll be to encourage the flower to hold a specific position. For this display, we convened a trio of identical, small-mouthed vases and placed just one or two stems in each, creating a tableau of clean lines and a few graceful arches.

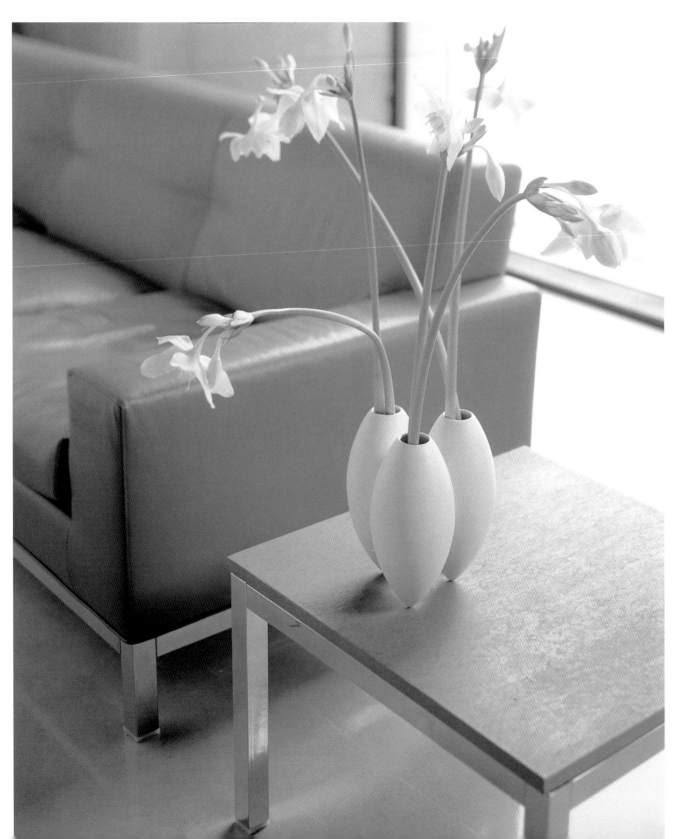

AAH, RESTRAINT. EXERCISING IT TAKES CONSCIOUS EFFORT—just ask anyone who's racing along at today's more-is-better pace. But as you can see here, it's worth it. Achieving this strikingly simple look requires that you limit yourself to just two tiny but effective design elements. First, place a minimal number of stripped-clean stems in a couple of clear containers that differ ever so slightly in size and shape. Then—this is as good as simplicity gets—make the water levels different in each.

HERE'S DELICATE BUT DEFINITE PROOF THAT A SIMPLE DISPLAY DOES NOT HAVE TO BE A STATIC ONE. By merely varying the lengths of your stems, you can give even a few flowers in individual bud vases a sense of movement and life. Some of the flower heads can sit right at the tops of the vase openings. Others can rise up above the rest or arch gracefully outward and down. Chances are, your flowers will be naturally inclined to fill specific roles. Pay attention to which are already tending toward a curved stature and which seem to want to stand tall, then cut and position them accordingly.

WHEN YOU'RE SWIRLING AROUND IN THE MIDST OF A SEASON THAT'S ALL ABOUT RIBBONS, BOWS, AND WRAPS, it's nice to let your flowers in on the celebration. This handful of elegantly packaged white calla lilies makes a sophisticated addition to a winter holiday display. Lay your lilies—or any type of flower with a head you want to protect—on a table or counter, so the heads dangle carefully over the edge. About halfway up their stems, wrap a ribbon several times, then tie it off in a knot or a simple bow. Trim off any excess from the base of the stems, so your flowers are the right height for your vase. Work gradually as you cut, trimming off only a small amount to begin with and standing the flowers in the vase to check the look. Remember, there's no way to add back height if you decide you need it later.

LET'S HEAR IT FOR DIVIDING AND CONQUERING.

One of the most obvious truths single-bloom displays tap into is that your flowers don't have to all congregate in one cluster to make an impression. We've filled this room with flowers by building visually on the windowsill bouquet. For an eye-catching central focus, we positioned three single stems at staggered heights on cake stands stacked on the coffee table. We then echoed the idea with paler blooms in more understated vases on two levels of the open bookshelf.

THIS IRREPRESSIBLY CHEERFUL DISPLAY IS AS MUCH OF A BREEZE TO ASSEMBLE AS YOU'D EXPECT. There's nothing more to it than gathering a bundle of same-colored, happy-go-lucky flowers (we used pink gerberas), and tucking them down, one by one, into a group of small-necked containers. A display like this also offers an ideal excuse for creating vases out of the pieces of a collection, whether they're cream bottles, table shakers, perfume bottles, or inkwells.

A LITTLE RUSTIC WRAPPING AND SOME COLORED-GLASS CONTAINERS are the main ingredients for these bouquets and displays in one. Lay your flowers on a flat surface, with their heads off the edge to protect them, and wrap the stems with a liberal amount of twine, thin rope, or raffia. For the full look we've created here, wrap just below the base of the flower heads. Finish by leaning your wrapped stems in place in your colored glass containers. If you want some added movement, alternate the direction in which each bouquet leans. Bonus: These charming little bundles make perfect favors when the party's over.

IF YOU'RE AT ALL CONCERNED THAT A FLOWER DISPLAY featuring just a few of a single flower type is in danger of looking dull, here's one designed to put your worries to rest. A bold combination of flower and container—tall, delicate wisps of white freesia and a heavy, rich-colored vase—give it its commanding presence.

COMBINATIONS

PUT ONE FLOWER NEXT TO ANOTHER. NOTICE HOW THE FUSCHIA LOOKS BRILLIANT AGAINST THE GOLD, OR HOW THE ABSTRACT SHAPE OF ONE IS STRIKING BESIDE THE TOWERING, STRAIGHT STALK OF THE OTHER, AND YOU'LL UNDERSTAND. *THIS* IS WHY MOST PEOPLE CAN'T HELP BUT GROUP FLOWERS TOGETHER INTO COMBINATIONS. THE KEY TO KEEPING THOSE COMBINATIONS FROM LOOKING LIKE CELLOPHANE-WRAPPED STORE BOUQUETS IS TO EXPERI- MENT WITH IMAGINATIVE MIXES OF COLOR, SHAPE, SIZE, AND TEXTURE, WORKING WITH BOTH FLOWERS AND FOLIAGE, FROM DECORATIVE GRASSES TO TROPI- CAL LEAVES.

in a sparkling white kitchen, for example, or a small bouquet of all-pink flowers in a powder-blue bathroom.

A second way to combine flower colors is to stay within the same general color family, blending yellow, orange, and apricot, say, or pink, purple, and blue. Just start with a base color, then add layers of harmonious shades. Color-family combinations are an effective way to create particular moods with flowers. Those on the warm side of the color wheel will tend to look full of zeal; cooler mixes come off as more calm and serene.

Finally—and most daring—mix colors that explode in a happy burst of high contrast. For combinations that are magnificent rather than simply mismatched, start with color pairs that occur in nature, but don't be afraid to experiment on the edges of color ranges. Maybe your version of red and green is flamingo pink and lime. Instead of lavender and peach, try magenta and bright orange.

COLOR

It's said that the human brain can perceive seven million different colors. If you find that a tad overwhelming, think of grouping flowers into three basic kinds of color combinations.

Mix a variety of flower types that are all the same shade, and you have the satisfying impact of a monochromatic arrangement. In addition to providing a strong presence, same-color combinations are especially easy to pair with a setting; picture an all-red arrangement

SHAPE

You have two general ways to go when you're putting together flower shapes. You can either stick with flower varieties that all have similar forms—maybe they're all delicate and round faced or all tall and goose-necked—so you end up with an arrangement that's basically uniform in shape. Or, you can mix two or more distinctly different shapes for a less symmetrical look.

TEXTURE

It's easy to be carried away by the flashier qualities of flowers and forget that a flower's soft, velvety petals or its prickly globes also have a lot to do with its personality. Creating interplay among flower textures is an especially imaginative way to bring a display to life. As with shape, you can emphasize either similarity or contrast when it comes to texture.

FOLIAGE

Willing to play the varied roles of peace-maker, supporter, and occasionally even co-star, foliage can be an indispensable part of a combination of flowers. It comes in colors ranging from deep purple to silver (not to mention many shades of green), making it the perfect solution for breaking up too-intense color combinations or blending those that aren't quite coming together. The thick stalks of some types of foliage help hold flower stems in place in a vase. The thin, grassy blades of others make natural ties or delicate filler. And broad leaves, spiraling branches, and other dramatic pieces can be featured parts of a combination.

IF YOU WERE WONDERING ABOUT RULES— *Does a "combination" require that all your flowers stand together in one vase? for example*—here's your answer. Gather together a group of similar-but-different containers; ours vary in shape and height, but share the same shade and texture. Then, divide your flowers among them. We filled one vase full with our most frilly flower, stood three tall blooms in another, let our most graphic flowers each have a vase to themselves, and filled the last one with nothing but a sprig of greenery.

THIS CELEBRATORY TABLE RUNNER JUST GOES TO SHOW, if you stick with a single color, you can combine any number of flower types and still end up with a harmonious display. Clear water glasses make fine containers for a table-long row of arrangements, especially if you're working with white. And here's the trick when you're playing with uniform color but various textures, sizes, and shapes: don't make each flower-filled glass a carbon copy of the others. Slightly varying the height and volume of each display makes the effect all the more enchanting.

YOU KNOW THE ETI-
QUETTE-BOOK RULE:
NEVER PUT FLOWERS
IN THE CENTER OF THE
TABLE THAT ARE TOO
TALL TO SEE OVER.
HERE'S AN EASY WAY
TO GAUGE THE
HEIGHT. REST YOUR
ELBOW ON THE TABLE,
THEN LET YOUR HAND
RELAX. IF THE FLOW-
ERS ARE TALLER THAN
YOUR WRIST, THEY'RE
TOO HIGH; GIVE THE
STEMS A SNIP.

WHILE EVERYONE ELSE IS DUTIFULLY FILLING A SINGLE VASE WITH ONE STEM OF WHITE, one stem of pink, one stem of white, one stem of pink, and so on, you can quietly grab a second container and give the tradition a twist. Separate your flowers into two containers, one per flower type, then combine them visually as bookends on a coffee table, dinner table, counter, or bar. With both batches of flowers here, we've left the leaves on the stems to create enough mass so the flowers stand securely in their wide containers—and to add to the luxuri-ousness of the look.

HERE'S PROOF THAT SUCCESSFUL FLORAL COMBINATIONS DO NOT REQUIRE BOUFFANT ARMLOADS OF EXPENSIVE BLOOMS. Playing off the colors of the table's dishes and linens and the painted coffee carafes we used as vases, we needed just six stems to create this vibrant display. If you're working with a limited budget, spend the bulk of it on a couple of exotic blooms, then set them off with a few other flowers that are more familiar—perhaps even plucked from the backyard.

AFICIONADOS OF TULIPS CAN TRULY APPRECIATE THE SUBTLE DISTINCTIONS in this combination of three layers of similar-but-different flowers. The rest of us are merely satisfied with the fact that they make a radiant display. We started with one variety of parrot tulip, cut the stems so the flower heads would just top the rim of the vase, then positioned them around the edge. Next, we cut the stems on a second variety so the flower heads would sit several inches above the first, and placed them behind the first row of tulips, crisscrossing their stems with the others for stability. Finally, we filled in the center with standard tulips, cut so they'd sit several inches higher than the second row.

WHEN YOU'RE USING CLEAR GLASS CONTAINERS, YOU WANT THE GLASS TO BE SPOTLESS AND THE WATER INSIDE SPARKLING—ESPECIALLY IF THE CONTAINERS DECORATE A FOOD TABLE.

SOMETIMES, YOU CAN SIMPLY TAKE A GOOD LOOK AT YOUR VASE or container before you ever choose a single flower, and it'll tell you about the kind of combination it needs. This vintage enamel pitcher, for example, calls for a bountiful spray of soft colors spilling out of its opening—we chose tulips, roses, and budding branches. To create a display with the same abundant appeal, set the branches in place first, then tuck in your flowers, positioning some in close to the center and allowing others to drape over the edge. Florists refer to this as creating "ins and outs." Whatever you call it, it's the perfect way to add fullness and dimension to a display.

SHAPE & SCALE

FLOWER DISPLAYS, LIKE PEOPLE, CAN BE STATUESQUE OR DIMINUTIVE, SLENDER OR ROUNDED, ANGULAR OR SOFT-EDGED, ASYMMETRIC OR PERFECTLY BALANCED. AND, AS WITH PEOPLE, MOST OF US LIKE VARIETY. MANY OF THE DIFFERENCES HAVE TO DO WITH THE FLOWERS THEM-SELVES—LET'S FACE IT, A BIRD OF PARADISE IS NEVER GOING TO LOOK DAINTY, AND IT'S DIFFICULT IF NOT IMPOSSIBLE TO MAKE A VIOLET TOWER OVER A TABLE SETTING. BUT YOU CAN ALSO DO MUCH TO GUIDE

THE SHAPE AND SCALE OF YOUR OVERALL DISPLAY BY HOW YOU CUT, COMBINE, AND CONTAIN YOUR FLOWERS.

SHAPE & SCALE

The flowers you choose to start with have a lot to do with the overall shape your arrangement takes. But no one ever said making those choices was going to be easy. Flowers—in all their many configurations—will force you to add words such as star, trumpet, cone, and snowflake to your mental list of basic shapes.

Forget that the result is often akin to fine art. The process of shaping a flower arrangement is actually quite logical. Cut a stem short and stick it in a small, squat vase, and you have a diminutive display. Leave it long and let it arch out of a tall, slender one, as we have here, and it becomes dramatic. The same basic reasoning applies to creating arrangements of any shape or scale. After you've chosen your flowers, it's all in how you cut and contain them.

If you're hosting a roomful of cocktail partiers, you might want one large, bold arrangement that stands out at the far end of the food table. For a more casual brunch for a few, perhaps small bouquets of pansies scattered around the table are better. A huge part of the battle of achieving the size and shape you want is choosing the right container. This wide-mouthed urn (left) encourages the hydrangeas it holds to form a full, generous mound, while the small-necked opening of the green vase (middle) cinches the roses into a more precise dome that echoes the rounded base. Unusual containers, such as this vase that rests on its side (right), can help remind you that flower arrangements don't have to stand up straight.

ONCE YOU REALIZE HOW EASY IT IS TO TWIST, TURN, or otherwise configure certain types of flowers and foliage, your options for shape expand. These rustic pockets of leaf and flowering vine are perfect examples. All you need to hold them together is a tiny amount of florist's tape and wire.

Form your leaf into a loose cone with a hole at the cone's base, and secure the wrap with a small piece of tape. Stick one end of the vine through the hole—so it, along with your leaf stem, can reach the water—then wind the rest of the vine in circles until it fills the cup of the cone. Secure the other end of the vine with a tiny piece of wire. If you like, add dried flowers and feathers as accents. Galax and banana leaves make good cones. Smaller leaves such as magnolia or ornamental cabbage are nice for individual arrangements. In the spring, fill your cones with sprays of Scotch broom or even flexible branches of forsythia. Try bittersweet in the fall.

IT'S ONE OF LIFE'S HAPPIEST MYSTERIES OF TIMING. Just when the thought of yet another chilly, dreary day becomes unbearable, the branches on the trees outside begin to bud. Bring them in and water them well, and you'll both be fooled into thinking spring has arrived early. Branches are sturdy enough to hold themselves in place in a heavy, deep vase. Place the shorter ones first, then thread the taller ones among them. Ours arranged themselves naturally into an arching, asymmetrical shape, which means centering the vase at the end of the table would have made it appear ready to fall to one side. The easy fix? We offset the vase just a bit. For more of a balanced fan shape, position straight cuttings in the middle of your vase, then fill in with curved branches at the edges, where they can dip and rise.

FORCING BLOOMS:

To force branches into bloom, use a sharp pair of pruning shears and wait until temperatures are above freezing to cut young branches that feature lots of plump flower buds. Condition the bottoms of the branches (see page 12), then place them in tepid water, put them in a cool spot such as the garage, and mist the buds regularly so they don't dry out. Once the buds start to bloom, move them to a bright location inside, but keep them out of direct sunlight.

MAYBE ALL YOU WANT TO DO IS SHOW OFF THE PLEASING SHAPE of the flowers you happen to have— without the distraction of foliage, a fancy vase, or any obvious arranging. In that case, strip the leaves from all your flower stems, group the stems in your hand so all the heads are at roughly the same height, cut the base of the stems evenly, place them in a large, clear vase, and lean them against one side. Keep the water level low in the vase so the stems aren't obscured—and to emphasize your minimalist approach.

OFTEN, TWEAKING A BASIC RULE IS ALL IT TAKES to transform a handful of flowers into an extraordinary display. Instead of standing them straight up in a vase, for example, let your flowers shoot out sideways, creating a dramatic, angular look. Use a shallow vase with a wide body and a small opening. Tuck the stems of your flowers into the widest part of the vase; its side and the lip of its opening will hold the angled flowers in place. If they need additional support, stick a wide, decorative leaf or two in beneath them. For extra effect, choose a vase that echoes the shape of your flowers, the way the rounded vase here accents the bulbous poppy pods and allium.

PERHAPS IT WAS THE FIRST HUMAN BEING EVER TO SPOT WATER LILIES floating in a pond who decided that flowers don't have to form towering sprays to be noticed. Since then, word has gotten around. Setting blossoms adrift in a low-edged vase, bowl, or dish is a wonderful way to weave flowers into all sorts of scenes, whether you want the look to be opulent (think gardenias and cut crystal), informal (maybe cornflowers in saucers), or something in between. Since their life spans are fairly short—typically a few hours—these are displays you want to assemble at the last minute. Use scissors to snip the blossoms cleanly from their stems, then set them on the surface of the water. You'll have the best luck with flattish flowers; three-dimensional blooms will tend to flip on their sides. If your flowers look as if they'd like companions, add greenery or floating candles to the display.

IF YOU DON'T HAPPEN TO OWN A BANQUET HALL, YOU PROBABLY WOULDN'T
decorate your table with flowers shooting out of the tops of oversized vases like these. But turn
the vases into sleek tabletop terrariums, and the look is clean, contemporary—and suited to
ordinary dining rooms. Hardy flowers not prone to early wilting do best tucked down inside a
container. Clean their stems of leaves, cut them so their heads will stand a couple of inches
below the container rim, then set them in place one by one, being careful not to crowd the
flowers too closely. They should appear to be willing accomplices with plenty of breathing room,
not captives pressing against the glass.

ONE OF THE LEAST COMPLICATED WAYS TO AFFECT THE SIZE AND SHAPE OF A VASE OF FLOWERS is to play with the length of the stems. To create this pot of nestled-together blooms, we cut the stems so the flowers would just peek over the top, then packed them in snugly. A tight grid of floral tape over the pot's opening helps hold them in place; see page 14 for instructions on how to tape one. Place single stems sparingly in the grid's openings, then fill in with more flowers until the look is as full as you'd like.

THERE'S ONLY ONE TRICK TO ASSEMBLING THIS EQUIVALENT OF A BUCKETFUL

OF FLOWERS from a country market: abandon any notion that less is more. Volume is the key to

creating bouquets this bountiful. You'll also need a generous-sized container. Buy tulips by the bunch

(you'll need at least two), clip an armload of peonies or hydrangea from the yard, or choose another

dense-petaled flower you can gather in great amounts. Hold the flowers up to your container and

cut the stems so the heads will spill out just above the container's lip, then fill the container until it's

brimming. The mass of stems and leaves do all the work of seeing that the display holds its shape.

CUTTING THESE IRISES SO THEY'RE SEVERAL FEET TALL, then placing each in its own dramatic, trumpet-shaped vase, sets them off like individual pieces of art. The imposing height and unadorned nature of the display—all stem-and-flower architecture and clear glass—pay homage to the details of the flowers themselves.

PURCHASE A FEW SMALL BOTTLE BRUSHES FOR CLEANING THE INSIDES OF YOUR SMALLER AND NARROWER VASES.

PICTURE THE MAJESTIC BLOSSOMS SHOWN HERE SNIPPED SHORT AND SITTING in the smaller white vases, and you have an immediate example of the power of scale. Though the shorter display would be perfectly beautiful, it would lack the impact, presence, and stark appeal of just a few lone stems slanted against the edges of giant clear tumblers.

IF YOU NEED TO CLEAN A CLEAR GLASS CON- TAINER THAT HAS AN OPENING TOO NARROW TO ACCOMMODATE EVEN A SMALL BOTTLE BRUSH, TRY SWISHING IT OUT WITH DENTURE CLEANER.

ASSEMBLING A FLOWER DISPLAY THIS TRANQUIL AND SERENE can absolutely stress you out if you start with the wrong vase. But choose one with a teeny, tiny opening that helps your flowers achieve perfect balance, and the rest of the job is pure meditative pleasure. Select one flower with some weight to it and another stalk or two of something willowy, then play with how you want to place them. The only rule is to make sure your highest point is not your heaviest, or your display will look as if it wants to tip.

THOUGH NOT PERFECTLY COIFED, THIS FRILLY SPRAY OF FRESH BABY'S BREATH has been shaped somewhat, so it's full and rounded rather than wild and woolly. To give your flowers the same treatment, start by shaping the display in your hand, creating a high point at what will be the center, then adding naturally flared sprigs around that point. Once you've shaped as many as you can hold, stand the flowers up to your container, determine how high you want the heads above the rim, cut the stems accordingly, then set the flowers in place. Fill in any gaps with additional sprigs, and finish by fluffing all the flowers gently, so the look is full and airy.

WHAT A WONDERFUL NEW WAY TO LOOK AT CARNATIONS—

which, by the way, are about one-third the cost of roses. These bound-together bouquets are also a pleasing study in contrasting shapes: tall, stately columns topped with billowing cupolas. They're easiest to assemble with two people working together. Begin with several flowers in the crook of your hand, then add more, circling the center at graduated heights, until you're holding about a dozen flowers that form a subtle dome. Have your partner wrap twine around the stems, beginning a few inches below the flower heads and crisscrossing it all the way down, then finish by tying it in a bow at the base.

POTTERY? YES. THIN BLOWN GLASS? FORGET IT. THE REAL SECRET BEHIND the popular look of combining a couple of heavy flowers featuring abstract shapes is to pick a super-sturdy pot to hold them. Otherwise, even if they don't topple over the minute someone breathes, everyone will be afraid they're about to—and the serenity you were striving for is lost. For an asymmetrical effect, cut the stem of your bigger, fatter bloom slightly shorter than the other.

FLOWERS DRINK MORE IN THE DARK. IF YOU NEED TO REVIVE A BOUQUET THAT HAS WILTED DURING A HOT COMMUTE HOME FROM THE FLOWER SHOP, GIVE THE STEMS A FRESH CUT AND PLACE THEM IN A BUCKET OF WATER IN A DARK ROOM, AND THEY'LL PERK RIGHT UP.

SURE, ANY THIN, NARROW VASE WOULD BE ABLE TO PERCH ITSELF ON THIS skinny windowsill and hold flowers—and we'd notice the display and think it pretty. But choose a tall-necked bottle vase and fill it with just a few graceful, far-reaching flower stalks, and the display deftly fills the length of the lower sill, making it so much more satisfying to see.

COLOR

WELL BEFORE THERE WERE PAINT CHIPS IN SHADES NAMED *ROSE* AND *JONQUIL* AND CRAYOLA

CRAYONS CALLED *PERIWINKLE* AND *VIOLET*, THERE WERE THE FLOWERS THEMSELVES, DOING

WHAT FLOWERS DO BEST: BRIGHTENING THEIR SURROUNDINGS. WHETHER YOU WANT A

VIBRANT BLEND OF HOT HUES, THE ELEGANT APPEAL OF MONOCHROME, OR 10 SLIGHTLY DIF-

FERENT SHADES OF BLUE, FLOWERS HAVE LONG BEEN ONE OF THE MOST VERSATILE, EFFECTIVE,

AND JUST PLAIN BEAUTIFUL WAYS TO BATHE A SPACE IN COLOR.

As you read this, people called hybridizers are hard at work, cultivating everything from midnight-blue roses to neon-green carnations, so you'll have them when your arrangement cries out for a new shade. If you're a purist who prefers the colors nature came up with, you'll still have no trouble finding a plentiful array.

If flowers were aware of what human beings think of them, they'd know our primary expectation is that they bring color into our lives. Which would explain why flowers get on so well with vases and other containers—those containers help ease some of the pressure. Containers can help strengthen a monochromatic look (below) or provide the contrast that makes a flower arrangement pop (above).

Of course, if you need them to, containers are also happy to fade into the background.

Flower colors have been used to symbolize virtues and sentiments for centuries—red roses: love and unity; white chrysanthemums: truth. But even if you don't know the symbolic meaning of every last sprig of purple heather (just for the record, it's solitude), using specific flower colors is a time-honored way to set a theme, establish a mood, or celebrate a season. This mix of orange, yellow, and russet, for example, makes a perfect fall harvest display. Combinations of pale yellow and blue—or all green—epitomize spring, while a pure-white bouquet accented with silvery-green foliage would provide a sparkling backdrop for champagne and noisemakers.

Set down even a single blossom in a vase, and notice how the colors in your walls, throw pillows, and even knickknacks suddenly perk up. Flowers are accustomed to having this sort of invigorating effect on their surroundings, so make the most of it. Experiment with flowers that play off the colors in your curtains, tablecloths, area rugs, or artwork.

THIS REFRESHINGLY SUBTLE COMBINATION OF COLOR JUST GOES TO SHOW that the winter holidays can mean much more than blaring reds and greens. We've gone with a more tranquil blend of snow-white topped with touches of crimson—and added interest by playing with balance, pairing heavy ceramic vases with delicate flowers that look as if they've just pushed their way up through a blanket of white.

FORGET COLOR WHEELS AND YOUR OLD ART-CLASS NOTES about value, saturation, and hue. Combining flower colors doesn't have to be any more complicated than choosing one bloom to stand out from the rest. In this case, we let a cluster of pale, pinkish-white poppies weave in and out of one another to form a soft backdrop, then added one poppy with a rich, ruddy shade that matches the wall behind it.

OKAY, CHANCES ARE, FLOWERS LIKE THESE AREN'T SPROUTING UP IN YOUR BACKYARD faster than you can pick them. But the good news, as you can see, is that you don't need many vibrant specialty blooms to create an exotic display. The key is to make bold color choices when it comes to both the flowers and their containers, then vary heights and shapes in your display. We divided our few number of blooms into two different-sized containers, choosing one that mimics the color of the flowers in the other.

SOMETIMES, YOU WANT A TABLE TO COME TO LIFE IN ONE BIG BURST OF COLOR. Other times, it's nice to spread the cheer around. We've opted for the second approach here, giving each place setting its own green-glass vase and filling it with shades of purple and yellow. The flower displays echo the colors of the table's linens and dishes, and dole them out in individual-size doses.

AS EVERYONE FROM PAINTERS TO FASHION DESIGNERS CAN TELL YOU, often the best way

to create a pleasing array of color is to layer one on top of the other. For this enchanting montage, we

started with a weathered wooden tray in shades of white and blue, followed with pink, blue, and white-

frosted drinking glasses and bottles, then added flowers in the same soft, pastel tones. We finished with a

few essential interlopers colored deep red and orange to give the whole display a zingy lift.

HERE'S A RAUCOUS GROUP OF FLOWERS THAT WASTES NO TIME getting the celebration underway. Well before the music is turned up and the bubbly drinks are poured, they're pulsing, radiating, and living it up. The multi-vase display is assembled with mostly easy-to-find, inexpensive flowers, with a few show-stoppers mixed in. The hot, brassy colors give the display its life-of-the-party personality, while the fact that no two vases are filled with the same combination makes each look as if it's ready to jump up and mingle.

SOME FLOWER DISPLAYS STAND UP AND TAKE CHARGE. Others work more quietly to help pull together a look. This subtle trio of light-green carnations is all it takes to reinforce the sparse style and citrus shade of the table setting. They, along with the accents of dried balls from sweet gum trees at each place, are also a good example of the fact that there's no need to overdo when you want to emphasize a color scheme.

IF YOU TAKE ONE LOOK AT THIS DISPLAY AND FIND YOURSELF—whatever the weather—feeling a cool breeze from a nearby window and longing for a glass of lemonade, you understand the effect that the color of a few flowers can have. This all-white arrangement of snowball-size hydrangea and airy Queen Anne's lace resting peacefully in a big vintage jar can make you nostalgic for summers past and take the heat off all at once.

THESE BLAZING SPRING BLOS-SOMS, POSING AS OVERFLOWING FROTH on the top of the world's most colorful martini set, would dare any gloomy guest not to smile and start having a good time. Meanwhile, they'll have everyone else kicking off their shoes and dancing. We used rhododendron and azalea blossoms for this display. Other full-bodied flowers such as hydrangea and peonies would create the same effect. Leave most of the leaves on your flowers when you first place them—they help support the blossoms—then edit them out a few at a time until you have the look you want.

CLEAN CONTAINERS ARE ONE OF THE BEST DEFENSES AGAINST BACTERIAL GROWTH (WHICH WILL CAUSE AN ARRANGEMENT TO FADE FAST). AFTER EACH USE, WASH YOUR FLOWER CONTAINERS WITH SOAPY WATER, RINSE THEM WITH BLEACH, AND DRY THEM THOROUGHLY.

SETTINGS

IF YOU'RE THE SORT OF PERSON WHO'S DRAWN TO CHICKEN-AND-EGG QUESTIONS, YOU COULD SPEND A LOT OF TIME PONDERING WHICH COMES FIRST, THE FLOWERS OR THE PLACE YOU'LL PUT THEM. YOU KNOW THAT ALL SORTS OF SETTINGS, FROM MANTELS AND DESKS TO WINDOWSILLS, READING TABLES, AND PORCH RAILINGS, BENEFIT FROM A SHOW OF FRESH BLOOMS. BUT DO YOU FOCUS FIRST ON THE SWEET PEAS CRYING TO BE CUT, THEN LOOK FOR THE BEST PLACE

FOR THEM? OR DO YOU START WITH THE EMPTY SPOT ON THE GUEST-ROOM DRESSER, THEN SEARCH FOR THE PERFECT FLOWER TO FILL IT? THE TRUTH, AS WITH MOST SUCH QUANDARIES, IS THAT YOU CAN MAKE A CASE EITHER WAY. SUCH PLEASANT AMBIGUITY, THIS BUSINESS OF PUTTING THE RIGHT FLOWERS IN THE RIGHT PLACE.

SOMETIMES, NARROWING DOWN THE SETTING FOR YOUR FLOWER DISPLAY to *dinner table* isn't quite specific enough. Questions still linger: *In the center?, At one end? Or how about individual posies at each place?* If you settle on the latter, make the displays look as if they're blooming out of each guest's dinnerware by topping the settings with bowls and nesting a short glass tumbler in each. Build the center of each bouquet in your hand, cut the flowers so the heads will just top the tumbler rim, set them in place, then fill in around the edges with more flowers cut to size. Be sure to fill each tumbler with enough flowers so the pressure of the packed stems holds each bouquet firmly in place.

ONE CHARMINGLY EFFECTIVE WAY TO INCORPORATE FLOWERS INTO ANY SETTING is to house them in a container that looks comfortably at home. This antique sideboard has been playing host to platters and bowls for decades, so we pressed one of the dishes into service as a vase for fresh garden cuts. A container this shallow won't do a good job of holding stems in place on its own, so use a frog or a piece of saturated floral foam in the bottom to anchor them, then let the blossoms overflow the edges.

A GIFT TABLE, A COCKTAIL-AND-APPETIZER STATION, AND THE CORNER OF A BAR are all places where it's fun to have your flower display as festively packaged as the pieces it shares space with. To dress the champagne table at this springtime fete, we wrapped bells of Ireland and lilies in an elegant white bag similar to those holding the nearby bottles of bubbly. Simply make sure your flowers are securely situated in a vase, then set it down inside a bag, tissue-lined box, or any similar wrap you have in mind.

A FEW WELL-CHOSEN PROPS—WITH FLOWERS AND GREENERY AS THE FOCUS— work together to turn this mantelpiece display into a welcome antidote to the season's overload of tinsel and blinking lights. We sprayed an inexpensive ceramic urn silver, then put a piece of saturated floral foam in its base to help hold the ends of a few single strands of greenery in place. Evergreen, holly, and magnolia are all good options for a low, wide arrangement like this one. Let the natural winding tendency of the greenery dictate your display's overall shape. Once the strands are secure, tuck in individual accent stems of colored berries and flowers. Placing a mirror behind the scene, which also includes greenery-wrapped candles and a few antique ornaments, doubles the display's subtle sparkle.

FOR MORE THAN A FEW OF US, HOSTING FRIENDS FOR DINNER THESE DAYS

MEANS takeout in front of the fireplace much more often than it means several courses at the dining room table. Here's an easy flower display that suits the times—and that won't hit everyone at eye level, even if they are sitting on floor cushions around the coffee table. It's as easy as cleanly snipping your flowers' stems down to a little less than an inch and floating the blossoms in a bowl of water. Some hardier blossoms, such as orchids, can last for up to a week this way; just change the water daily and give the stems a fresh cut each time you do.

DURING CERTAIN TIMES OF YEAR—particularly when gardens and farmers' markets are overflowing outside—nothing will do but to have every surface inside erupting with flowers as well. Bathroom counters, study shelves, and tucked-away end tables all must sport their own signs of summer life. What's best about these displays is how casual they can be in terms of flowers, containers, and technique. We filled this ordinary tin pail with an unpretentious bunch of daisies and small spray roses, using nothing more than the flowers' own foliage to hold everything in place.

FLOWERS WITH LOTS OF UNRULY FOLIAGE (WHICH YOU MAY WANT TO KEEP FOR CERTAIN LOOKS) CAN BECOME TANGLED UP WITH ONE ANOTHER IN THEIR PREP CONTAINER. EVERY TIME YOU TRY TO PICK OUT A SINGLE STEM TO ADD TO THE ARRANGEMENT YOU'RE SHAPING IN YOUR HAND, A DOZEN OTHERS COME OUT OF THE WATER WITH IT. THE SOLUTION IS TO UNTANGLE ALL THE FLOWERS FIRST, AND LAY THEM OUT FLAT ON A WORKTABLE.

EVEN WHEN YOU'RE WORKING WITH SOMETHING AS STANDARD AS A TABLETOP, you've got several options regarding exactly *where* to put your flowers. On top of vines or branches that wind down the center of the table is a lovely one. Settle your runner in place first. We've used birch branches here; bittersweet and grapevine would both work well, too. Or, for a richer look, try ivy. Pull apart little pockets in the runner where you can hide tiny jars, positioning them in a loose zigzag pattern. Fill the jars with water, then stick a flower in each. If your jars are different heights, place your heavier blossoms in the shorter ones. Finish by decorating each plate with a snipped flower head just before everyone sits down.

FOR SOME HAPPY REASON, NO ONE EVER THINKS OF IT AS OVERKILL

to gather a bunch of flowers together and put them on display right in the middle of their own out-side environment—so they show up everywhere from picnic tables to deck rails. Here's a breezy display idea that's right in keeping with the carefree style of outdoor settings. Lay the flowers on their sides in a big platter or shallow bowl, as if they're lazily lounging around. To hold them there, cover the base of their stems with a few handfuls of crushed or cubed ice.

YOU'RE NOT TRYING TO COMPETE WITH THE JAPANESE MASTERS

who consider formal flower arranging a spiritual art, but you do like the idea of achieving harmony and balance. So, try this simplest of walking meditations. Go outside and pick a small handful of whatever happens to be blooming. Bring the bouquet in, and give it a home in a container that looks at ease beside your bathroom toothbrush holder or bedside water glass. Stand back and let the tranquility take over.

ADMIT IT. IF IT'S ONLY THE IMMEDIATE FAMILY, you serve yourselves from pots and pans on the stove. On the special days when others join you, it's easiest to simply modify the habit, and set up a buffet. A charmingly appropriate way to add flowers to a help-yourself setting is to let them drape out of their own serving bowl. This footed bowl works especially well, because it elevates the display. Placing an unfooted bowl on top of a pedestal cake stand would produce the same results. Allow your flowers to fall loosely to one side, holding their stems in place with glass marbles or with weights better suited to the setting, such as berries, fruit, or, in this case, maybe boiled eggs still in their shells.

IF YOU WANT YOUR FLOWERS TO LOOK JUST SO FOR A SPE- CIFIC OCCASION, HERE ARE SOME LAST-MINUTE TWEAKING TIPS. TO GET BLOOMS TO OPEN MORE FULLY, PUT THE FLOWERS IN WARM WATER AND POSITION THEM IN A SUNNY SPOT. ONCE THEY'VE OPENED UP, TRANSFER THEM TO COLD WATER AND A COOL, DARK LOCATION UNTIL IT'S TIME TO PULL THEM OUT FOR THE PARTY. TO SLOW DOWN THE OPENING OF FLOW- ERS THAT PEAK TOO SOON, GO STRAIGHT TO THE COLD WATER AND A COOL, DARK LOCATION.

IT MAKES SENSE THAT A PLACE WE DECORATE WITH ARTWORK AND LIGHTS would also welcome fresh flowers. Walls—outfitted with any sort of holding stand—are a wonderful location for simple flower displays. Here, we've turned a wall-mount candle stand into the per- fect spot for a small glass tumbler holding a few bright stalks of flowers. A couple of decorative shelf brackets hung side by side could perform the same function. This easy idea is especially suited to nooks, crannies, and the thin sec- tions of walls between windows and doors.

THE DISSIMILAR IMAGES OF *FLOWER* AND *SUCTION CUP* HAVE LIKELY NEVER

entered your mind at the same time until now. But put the two together, and mirror faces, windowpanes, and any other vertical surface the cup can grip become spots for hanging bud vases. Buy a suction cup already equipped with a hook at a craft or home improvement store, and stick it in place. Remove the labels from a small, lightweight bottle or jar, wrap its neck with thin craft wire, and twist the end of the wire into a loop to hang from the suction cup's hook. Make several for a tiered series of hanging vases.

CONTAINERS

THINK OF VASES AND OTHER
CONTAINERS AS ATTIRE FOR
YOUR FLOWERS. ON CERTAIN
OCCASIONS, YOU WANT TO
OUTFIT THEM IN SOMETHING
CLASSIC AND SUBTLE. OTHER
TIMES, YOU WANT A FLASHY
COSTUME. NO MATTER WHAT,
YOU WANT OUTERWEAR THAT
HELPS THE FLOWERS HOLD
THEIR SHAPE. AS WITH ANY
WARDROBE, IT'S USEFUL TO
OWN A GOOD COLLECTION
OF BASIC PIECES PLUS A FEW
SPECIALTY ITEMS THAT ADD
COLOR AND FLAIR.

Choosing the right container for the right bouquet is the key to pulling off today's most popular look: flowers that appear to have been effortlessly tossed into a vase—yet never droop, flop, sink, or fall open on both sides, leaving a gaping space in the middle. Here's a look at basic vase shapes and what they do best.

CONTAINERS

TALL & THIN

Whether they're cylindrical or square, tall, thin vases create arrangements with a clean, contemporary look. They're best for holding straight, sturdy stems that match the lines of the vase. You can use them to contain just a few flowers, but may need to add marbles, rocks, or some other form of frog in the bottom to help hold the flowers in place. For an especially straight-lined look, go with a tightly packed bunch of flowers, cut all the stems the same length, and let the thin vase hold them together in a tight mass.

LOW & ROUND

Dinner tables (not to mention dinner guests) crave these shallow-but-attractive containers that don't interfere with conversation or sightlines. Low, round vases with narrower openings are nice for tight, dome-shaped arrangements. If you have one with a wide mouth, try floating flowers inside it. Both narrow and wide-mouthed versions are good bases for branching stems with big blossoms, such as lilies or peonies. The stems can crisscross inside the vase, to provide stability, and the blossoms can balance just beyond the edge of the opening.

FLARED

Vases that are narrower at their base than at their mouth, whether the flare is slight or full blown, are meant for abundant arrangements. The shape encourages open, fan-shaped displays best assembled with stiff-stemmed flowers. The wider the flared mouth of your vase, the more important it is that you fill it with generous-sized blossoms that gently spread when you gather the stems. If you use daintier buds, the top of the arrangement may look thin.

RECTANGULAR & SQUARE

Short and wide straight-sided vases (as opposed to the tall, thin versions) open up arrangements. That means they're not a good choice for holding just a few stems of flowers, which tend to look skimpy and tilt to one side or the other in all the open space. Flowering branches or vines that twist and curve in horizontal directions do especially well in this vase shape. You can also use foliage to help any kind of flower conform to the geometric space.

URN

This classic shape features a wide body topped with a narrow neck. It's that neck that gives you a great deal of control over how the flowers you put in the vase behave. Even those that naturally like to droop will get the support they need if you don't leave the stems too long. Domed bouquets that echo the form of the urn's globe-shaped base are the traditional choice for this style of vase—they complete the elegant, hourglass effect.

BUD & POSY

Vases that are narrow enough to keep a single stem from wavering or diminutive enough to look full when they're holding only a few blossoms are an important part of a basic collection. They epitomize simple flower style, encouraging you to go ahead and display flowers even if you don't happen to have an entire bouquet. And they're indispensable as containers when it comes to salvaging the few still-fresh blooms of an otherwise tired arrangement.

BEYOND BASICS

Once you've got the basic vase shapes you need to create the looks you like, embellish your collection with pieces that emphasize color, unusual materials, and even variations on the traditional forms. Finally, keep in mind that virtually anything that will hold water can be transformed into a vase. In the pages that follow, you'll see that objects as unlikely as egg shells and old-fashioned mail slots make fine flower containers.

A CONTAINER CAN HELP BRING A FLOWER DISPLAY TO LIFE through the contrast it provides: a black vase holding ruby-red flowers; a squat, round bowl filled with statuesque stalks; or, in this case, a stout, rugged, earthenware pot holding a dainty bunch of delicate hyacinth sprigs. When you use ceramic pieces as flower vases, be sure the ones you choose are glazed, making them watertight. Water will seep out of unglazed pots and also out of stone vases and urns meant for outdoor use.

THE HUMBLEST OF COMMON WILDFLOWERS COULD LOOK EXOTIC peeking over the top of their own bamboo forest. Mail-order companies sell the bamboo you'll need to create your own set of standing containers like these. Some well-stocked florists may be able to order it, too. It comes by the pole and should be several inches in diameter. Use a fine-toothed saw to cut the bamboo pole into the lengths you want, then hollow each piece, using a stick to break through the thin diaphragm at each joint. Stand the hollow pieces in a deepish tray with a lip, add pebbles or marbles to help hold the bamboo upright, if necessary, and fill the tray with water. Cut your flowers so their heads will just top the openings of their bamboo vases and their stems will reach the water in the tray.

ONE OF THE EASIEST WAYS TO MAKE A SIMPLE FLOWER DISPLAY

STRIKING is to put it in an unexpected—or at least less common—place. A thin, narrow container like this one lends itself to all sorts of under-adorned locations, from the space behind the bathroom sink to the headboard of a bed. Its suction-cup feet allow it to hold on in tricky spots.

THERE'S MUCH TO BE SAID FOR A MINIMALIST POT LIKE THIS ONE.
Rather than ornate shape and detailed design, it offers a rich, earthy texture that makes it a
perfect base for natural displays that incorporate herbs, seed pods, grasses, and branches.
And its narrow-necked opening makes it the easiest container type to work with if you
have thin-stemmed flowers whose direction you want to control.

ANYONE WHO HAS EVER PUT ON A BLOUSE, FOLLOWED BY A VEST, followed by a silk scarf—then received compliments all day long—understands the benefits of layering. You can add texture and interest to a flower display in the same way. We've used the technique here, beginning with a bottom layer of a big woven basket, then adding small porcelain vessels holding orchid sprays. To give the display an extra bit of dimension, we chose porcelain pieces that vary in height.

BULBOUS FLOWERS SUCH AS EARLY TULIPS AND DAFFODILS DRINK ONLY FROM THE GREEN PORTION OF THEIR STEMS, SO SCRAPE AWAY THE WHITE PARTS OF THE STEM ENDS BEFORE PLACING THEM IN WATER.

OFTEN, ESPECIALLY WITH A FOCAL-POINT DISPLAY such as the centerpiece here, your flowers and container can be the key to tying together a larger look. For this table setting, we wanted to create a rustic, homespun atmosphere that didn't drift into all-out country. The clean-lined tin coffeepot filled with cotton blossoms and witch hazel helps reinforce the setting's soothing colors and no-frills approach.

THESE CASUALLY MIXED COMBINATIONS OF PINK AND RED TULIPS are peeking up out of the hollow centers of ceramic chimney flues. Inside the flues, the tulips are sitting in standard vases full of water. You can use the same approach to make flowers look as if they're blooming out of any number of unlikely containers, from wooden wine crates to oversized shopping bags.

DELICATE SYMBOLS OF LIFE ITSELF, EGGS HAVE LONG REPRESENTED the spirit of spring. This makes them perfect plate-side containers for tiny handfuls of early buds. For each display, crack an egg, break off the top, and wash the inside of the larger portion of the shell. Pull flowerets off blooming plants, stick them down into the eggshell container, and fill the shell with water to the rim. Set your finished displays down in eggcups. If you happen to have a collection of colorful or vintage eggcups you'd like to show off, all the better.

IF YOU HAVE SMALL POSIES TO CONTAIN, ONE OPTION IS TO SIMPLY WRAP THEM UP in raffia-tied leaves. The resulting pretty packages make delightful table decorations that are easy for guests to take home as gifts. For each, start by bundling a small amount of thin-stemmed flowers. Hold the stems together with a rubber band, then cut them so the flowers are approximately 3 inches (7.6 cm) tall. Numerous types of leaves will work as wraps. Consider magnolia, laurel, fig, or grape leaves, or any good-sized leaf from a houseplant. Oil your leaf with vegetable oil if it's stiff, put a wet piece of paper towel in its center (where the flowers' stems will be), then wrap it around the stems and secure the top of the wrap with a length of raffia.

SOME CELEBRATIONS CALL FOR HEARTY, ROBUST EVERYTHING, from food and drink to laughter. The last thing you want in the middle of any such unrestrained party is a slender crystal vase. Instead, try turning a heavy, deep serving bowl into the foundation for a floating bouquet. Choose one with a big well and a wide opening, so you can load it up with a vigorous combination of textures, colors, and shapes. Snip your flowers' stems down to a little less than an inch to start, then give them a fresh cut and refill the bowl with fresh water daily to keep the display lively for several days.

VINEGAR BOTTLES, OLIVE OIL BOTTLES, WINE AND IMPORTED WATER BOTTLES—
it's highly possible you'd have to look no farther than your recycling bin to come up with a collection of colored glass you could line up in the sunlight and fill with flowers. Clean the bottles and remove the labels (unless yours feature colorful logos you like). For added interest, cut the tops off a few, as we have here. You can buy a bottle cutter at any craft store; just run the tool around the bottle's neck, then tap the top piece and pull it off. To keep the heavy-headed gerberas we used here from drooping, we wired the stems. Page 11 tells you how.

FINDING A FLOWER CONTAINER THAT'S SLIGHT-LY OUT OF THE ORDINARY is often as easy as experimenting with materials other than clear glass. These white porcelain plant buckets are just the right touch in this bright, airy setting. In a more modern environment, you might try chrome kitchen canisters or a black plastic desk organizer with lots of tall, vertical slots. Want something more folksy? Pull out your collection of pewter beer steins.

THE MORE CAREFREE THE CONTAINER, IT SEEMS, THE EASIER IT IS to let go of any flower-arranging notions that have to do with symmetry, uniformity, and perfect balance. Filling these basic water glasses with blooms of different sizes and with different numbers of blooms is what gives the casual display its charm. The subtle etched spirals on the glasses add just a touch of movement.

IF YOU WANT TO ETCH YOUR OWN GLASS FLOWER CONTAINERS, NON-ACID ETCHING CREAMS AND LIQUIDS, AVAILABLE AT CRAFT STORES, MAKE IT EASY. YOU APPLY THEM TO YOUR GLASS USING EITHER STENCILS OR A FREEHAND DESIGN, THEN WASH THEM OFF MINUTES LATER. THEY LEAVE BEHIND AN EVEN, FROSTED, PERMANENT FINISH.

**SO YOU DON'T OWN A VILLA
IN THE HILLS OF TUSCANY.**
So what. Go ahead and move a big
stone or ceramic garden urn inside,
let flowers tumble out of the top,
and pretend. Outdoor pots are typically porous and have a drainage
hole in the bottom, so to turn them
into indoor containers for fresh
flowers, you need to stick a vase
down inside the body. Flowers featuring a good amount of mass and
weight look best in these hearty,
heavy containers. The smaller vase
inside will help you control the
shape of the bouquet.

**ROSES WILL LAST LONGER IF
YOU REMOVE THE THORNS
AND MOST OF THE LEAVES
FROM THEIR STEMS, THEN
SPLIT THE ENDS OF THE
STEMS (SEE PAGE 12) BEFORE
PLACING THEM IN WATER.
PARE THE THORNS WITH A
SHARP KNIFE, WORKING FROM
THE TOP DOWN.**

IN THE DAYS BEFORE PLASTIC BINS AND CARDBOARD BOXES, people were more likely to create storage containers that both looked good and lasted. That means those items are often still around and still presentable. Shop flea markets and auctions for pieces that once sorted mail, organized tools, or stored kitchen utensils, and turn them into one-of-a-kind vases. We placed small glass jars filled with water in the bottom of each of the mail slots on this vertical strip, wrapped bouquets in wax paper for a bit of added texture, then stuck a bouquet into each slot. If you're working with a container with a series of openings, other options would be to play with a gradation of flower colors in each, or start with a small bouquet at one end and work up to a large one in the final opening.

IF YOU'RE LOOKING FOR AN EASY BUT INVENTIVE WAY TO INCORPORATE FLOWERS INTO A PARTY THEME, this is it. We've used daffodils in kerchiefs for a springtime brunch, but you could just as easily tie on bandannas filled with daisies for a summer cookout or baby bonnets and sweet peas for a shower for a mother-to-be. Use a rubber band or string to fix your flowers into small posies, stick the stems into small plastic bags filled with water, and tie off the tops of the bags with twist ties. Tie your holders onto the backs of chairs, so each forms a pocket for a bundle of flowers. The weight of the water in the bags should hold the flowers in place, allowing them to peek out the ends of the pockets. If not, add a few marbles inside the bags.

PAY ATTENTION, AND CERTAIN FLOWERS WILL TELL YOU THERE'S NO WAY they're going to be happy in anything that reminds them even remotely of a traditional-looking vase. These gleeful little ball-shaped blooms known as crespidia are just such flowers. To satisfy their natural inclination to frolic about a table, we stood them in the glasses of a vodka chiller set. They're free, this way, to scatter themselves to individual place settings or, in moments of solidarity, to gather in the set's ice bucket filled with marbles.

WHAT COULD BE BETTER THAN A SIMPLE FLOWER DISPLAY THAT ALSO HARKENS BACK TO SIMPLER TIMES? Flea markets and antique shops are your best sources for the containers you need to create them. This wooden crate studded with vintage soda bottles, for example, can take you right back to the childhood porch where you ate Popsicles with your favorite cousins, even if your summers these days consist mainly of traffic-filled commutes and weekend yard work. For similar looks, try milk bottles in an antique milk carrier or Mason jars in a berry basket.

HANDMADE POTTERY BOWLS FEATURING VIBRANT SPLASHES OF PATTERN AND COLOR have become wildly popular items to collect—and even to create at do-it-yourself ceramics studios. If you happen to have a couple you'd like to show off, they make delightful bases for blooming bulbs you've forced indoors. Fill each bowl approximately three-quarters full with potting soil, plant your bulbs, and water them well, keeping them moist throughout the forcing period. Place the planted bulbs in a cool, dark area, such as a garage. They'll root in about 10 to 12 weeks, depending on the type of bulb, and develop sprouts several weeks later. When the shoots are several inches tall, move the bowls to a location with low light and slightly warmer temperatures for a few days, then out to a sunny location where the bulbs can bloom.

HOLDING IT ALL TOGETHER

Experiment with today's simple approach to displaying flowers, and you'll realize something: there's casual and unadorned, and then there's just plain sloppy. The difference typically has to do with how well everything is held together. Often, the right container is all you need. But other times, your flowers require a bit more help—even if all they're supposed to do is assume a natural and carefree pose. Fortunately, the help comes in the form of basic, easy-to-use props, from frogs and pebbles to marbles and ribbon. You can either hide these holding devices down in a vase, or, as we have in this chapter, use them as a featured part of your display.

Various holding devices: flower frogs, marbles, rocks, cranberries, and chicken wire

FLOWER FROGS

No one seems to know exactly how these handy little ornaments acquired the same name as the amphibian known for leaping about—maybe it's that they're both at home in water—but once you discover the virtues of flower frogs, you won't care what they're called. As delightful to look at as they are useful, they come in versions featuring thin pins, deep wells, metal-mesh grids, and fanciful wire twists, and they're made of everything from china to colored glass. All are designed to secure the ends of cut blossoms. You'll find new ones for sale at flower and garden shops. Vintage versions, available at flea markets and antique shops, are now popular collectors' items.

MARBLES & ORNAMENTAL STONES

Match the material to the size and weight of your flower stems, and many types of small objects can anchor flowers in place in the bottom of a clear vase. Colored marbles and ornamental stones are sold by the bag for just this purpose. Beads, shells, shards of beach glass, and pieces of broken china would all work, too.

BERRIES & FRUITS

While performing the same function as marbles or stones, berries and fruits can also add a dash of seasonal

Ribbons, raffia, and leaves can all serve as wraps for arrangements.

flair to a flower display. Try cranberries at the holidays, or maybe whole lemons holding in place the thick stems of sunflowers in an arrangement celebrating the height of summer.

TIES

Whether you're motivated by form, function, or a combination of the two, sometimes it's a nice twist to tie flowers together into bundles before placing them in a vase. You can use ribbon, raffia, rope, twine, even wire to create interestingly bound bunches.

LEAVES

Take the tying of bundles one step further, and package your flowers in a natural wrap. You can order large, tropical leaves from

florists, and may be able to purchase leaves such as banana leaves at a well-stocked produce market. But don't feel you must have something particularly exotic. You simply need leaves that are medium to large in size and reasonably tough.

CHICKEN WIRE

The most basic and least flashy holding device for flowers is nothing more than a carefully wadded ball of chicken wire—the kind you can find at any hardware store or home improvement center. Its wide mesh provides convenient slots for sticking in flower stems. The problem with chicken wire is that it looks like…chicken wire. Unlike other holding solutions, this is one you'll want to cover up by tucking it well inside an opaque vase.

THOUGH THIS DISPLAY OF COMPLETELY SUBMERGED FLOWERS is not one you can count on having around for days and days, it does make a fabulous focal point for a dinner party or other event—complete with effervescent air bubbles that form around the flower as oxygen surfaces from the water. To weight down these spray roses with rocks, we crisscrossed a length of thin wire around each rock, secured the wire with a twist, then wound the wire around the bottom of the rose's stem, leaving a bit of space between the rock and the stem, so each flower appears to float. Matching flower and container size is important for this display. You want the fit to be neat, but should avoid a container so narrow that the flowers press up against the glass.

WITHOUT SOMETHING TO HOLD THEM IN PLACE, the stems of these holiday-red amaryllis would simply dangle in the wide flutes we've chosen for this display. But filling the flutes first with crab apples helps the stems maintain the gentle twist that gives the arrangement its shape. Fresh cranberries would do the same job—and also accent the red blooms. Depending on your container, color scheme, and the season you're celebrating, you can use everything from orange and lime wedges to grapes or blanched almonds to give your flower stems a place to anchor in a vase. For an added touch, we hooked a thin wire strung with crystals to the lip of each vase, and twisted it around the base. Beaded wire would give a display a less formal look.

CLUSTERING YOUR FLOW-ERS INTO BOUND BOU-QUETS IS AN INTERESTING WAY TO DISPLAY THEM— not to mention deliver them as gifts. Wrapping those bouquets in fresh leaves makes them all the more memorable. Form your flower bouquet in your hand, leaving all the stems long; trim them only to make sure they're even. Secure the stems with a rubber band, then lay the bouquet in the center of the leaf. Overlap the sides of the leaf around the stems, and secure the wrap with twine, ribbon, raffia, even wire. You want the stems to stick out past the base of the wrap, so they can easily reach the water once you set the flowers in a container. Also, be sure not to wrap your flowers too tightly; leave them room to open, if necessary, and breathe.

BLEACHED ROCKS AND THIN ROPE COLLABORATE TO HOLD THESE FOLKSY, FLOWERS-UNDER-GLASS BOUQUETS in place. Size is important when matching flowers and containers for a display of this kind; you want the flowers to fill the space inside the containers, but you don't want the flower faces pressed up against the glass. For each, build a bouquet in your hand, using buds in the middle and filling in with full blooms around the outside. Add a rubber band around the stems near the base of the heads, lay the bouquet on a counter, with the heads off the edge to protect them, wrap a length of thin rope around the rubber band several times, and tie it off. Cut the stems so the flower heads stand below the container opening, hold the bouquet in place in the center of the container, fill in the base with rocks until the bouquet can stand on its own, then add water.

WE'VE RESTRAINED OURSELVES HERE, CREATING A COOL, WINTERY DISPLAY using clear bubble-glass paperweights and realistic-looking plastic freezable cubes—the kind kitchen stores sell as "designer ice"—to hold a few stems of white flowers in place. But the possibilities for variations on this theme range from colorful to kitschy. The freezable cubes come in bright balls and tropical fish styles, to name just a few. And a collection of vintage snow globes would make fine substitutes for these more classic-looking paperweights. Fill the base of your container with the cubes and weights first, add water, then secure single flower stems in place. If you want to use an oversize container, as we have here, cut the flowers so they don't reach the rim.

WHITE FLOWERS BRUISE ESPECIALLY EASILY. HANDLE THEM WITH EXTRA CARE—AND AS LITTLE AS POSSIBLE.

Contributors

These two talented artists helped develop the book's content and created a number of the flower arrangements featured.

Josena Aiello-Bader has been a floral designer for more than 20 years, creating arrangements for shops, set dressings for Warner Brothers, and displays for Biltmore Estate in Asheville, North Carolina. Currently, she's the manager of The Gardener's Corner, a flower shop also in Asheville.

Kenneth Trumbauer has worked in the field of visual merchandising since the mid-1980s. In addition to handling freelance projects for numerous clients, he has worked with retailers such as Saks Fifth Avenue, Pier 1 Imports, Neiman Marcus, and Biltmore Estate in Asheville, North Carolina.

A rose to:

• Cynthia and Joe Kimmel, for opening up their lovely home and patios to our cameras.

• Mary "Bee" and Molly Seiburg of The Gardener's Corner/Gardener's Cottage, both in Asheville, North Carolina, for supplying many of the flowers and containers that appear in the book.

Index

Amaryllis, 22, 131

Azalea blossoms, 74

Baby's breath, 58

Bamboo, 94

Banana leaves, 46

Bells of Ireland, 80

Bouquets, 31, 102, 123, 125

Branches, 84

Bulbs, 23, 115

Buying and caring for flowers, 11, 18

Calla lilies,

Carnations, 59, 72

Chicken wire, 10, 118

Color, 63-75

Combinations, 33-42
    color, 34; foliage, 35
    texture, 35
    shape and scale, 35, 43-62

Conditioning, 11

Containers, 90
    Types of, 91-93; Care, 19

Cotton blossoms, 100

Crespidia, 112

Cutting, 11
    Tools, 10

Daffodils, 110

Daisies, 110

Eggshells, 103

Exotics, 39

Feeding and watering, 12

Fig leaves, 102

Floating flowers, 50, 82, 104, 119

Floral foam, 10

Florist's tape, 10, 52

Florist's wire, 10

Flower frogs, 10, 117

Forcing
    bulbs, 23; flowers, 19, 46

Forming arrangements, 14-17

Forsythia, 46

Freesia, 32

Galax, 46

Gerberas, 30, 105

Grape leaves, 102

Hydrangea, 72

Holding devices, 10, 116-118

Laurel, 102

Lilies, 80

Irises, 55

Magnolia, 46, 103

Marigolds, 24

Ornamental cabbage, 46

Poppies, 67

Queen Anne's lace, 72

Rhododendron blossoms, 74

Roses, 31, 108

Scotch broom, 46

Settings, 76

Shape and scale, 43-62

Single blooms, 21-32

Stem grids, 14-15

Straightening stems, 13

Table runner, 37

Treating stems, 12

Tulips, 40-41, 53, 101

Water mister, 10

Wilted flowers, 13

Witch Hazel, 100

Wrapping bundles, 31, 102, 123, 125

7/12/02   15 71/24 95

7/12/02   15 71/24 95